Birds
to Spot

Illustrated by Stephanie Fizer Coleman

Designed by Jenny Brown

Words by Sam Smith and
Kirsteen Robson

You can use the stickers to fill in the chart
at the back of the book, so you can keep
track of the birds you have seen.

Garden birds

Goldfinch
Has a bouncy flight and a twittering song. Feeds in flocks on small seeds.

Female is light brown rather than red.

Bullfinch
Found in hedges and on edges of woods. Its call is a soft 'pee-ew'.

Chaffinch
The rhythm of its song sounds like, 'Sweet, sweet, sweet. Pretty lovey, meet me here'. Female's head and body are light brown.

Often seen in flocks on farmland in winter.

Greenfinch
Seen especially in winter.
In spring, it calls with a
wheezy 'dweep'.

Broad black band
on chest.

Blue tit
Listen for its
'tsee-tsee-tsee'
and 'churrr' calls.

Young have
paler feathers.

Great tit
Lives in woodlands and
gardens. Its song sounds
like 'tea-cher tea-cher'.

3

Garden birds

Song thrush
Has a loud, warbling song. Often seen breaking open snail shells on rocks.

Dunnock
Feeds under bird tables. Mouse-like walk. Often flicks wings.

Robin
Male and female both sing, even in winter, with a long whistle followed by a liquid warbling. Its alarm call is 'tic-tic'.

4

Female is sooty brown.

Blackbird

Male often sings its loud, musical song at sunrise or sunset. Clucking alarm call.

Wren

Very small. Loud, warbling song ends with a powerful trill. Never stays still for long. Scuttles like a mouse.

Collared dove

Found in large gardens, parks or near farm buildings. Repeats a loud 'cooo-coo-coo' call.

Town birds

Feral pigeon
Very common in towns
and cities. Breeds on ledges.
Eats seeds and scraps.

Starling
Often flies in huge, swirling flocks at
dusk. Mimics songs of other birds, and
sounds such as phones or car alarms.

House sparrow
Lives wherever there are
people. Often seen in flocks.
Noisy 'cheep cheep' call.

Long tail very noticeable in flight.

Magpie

Found in parks, gardens, farmland and woods. Loud 'chacker-chacker' call.

Short tail is forked.

Swift

Seen on summer evenings from May to August. Flies fast, often in flocks, catching insects. Screaming call.

Pied wagtail

Wags tail as it walks, bobs up and down as it flies. Cheery 'chi-zick' call.

Woodland birds

Look for white bottom in flight.

Jay
Often hides in trees and sometimes visits gardens. Call is a harsh 'skairk, skaird'.

Blackcap
Moves from perch to perch singing its chattering song. Alarm call sounds like pebbles tapping together.

Female's cap is brown.

Willow warbler
Seen in summer. Its pale legs and high-to-low song help to tell it apart from a chiffchaff.

Nightingale
Listen for its powerful,
melodic song in May
and June.

Great spotted woodpecker
Size of a blackbird. Drums with its
beak on trees in spring, in short
bursts that rise and fade.

Green woodpecker
Pigeon-sized. Often feeds on
the ground. Has a laugh-like
'glug, glug, glug' call.

Woodland birds

Nests in tree-holes.

Nuthatch
Very short tail. Climbs
up and down trees in a
series of short hops.

Coal tit
Likes conifer woods but often
seen in deciduous trees too.
Large white patch on back of head.

Long-tailed tit
Look for groups of these birds in
hedgerows and edges of woods.
Listen for their 'see see see' call.

Jackdaw

Found near old trees, old buildings, or cliffs. Nests in colonies.

Carrion crow

More often seen alone or in pairs. Eats lots of things, including dead meat. Has a deep, harsh 'kraa-kraa' call.

Treecreeper

Climbs up tree trunks and flies down again to search for food. High-pitched call.

Farmland birds

House martin

Summer visitor found
in country and towns.
Catches insects in flight.

Builds cup-shaped nests
under edges of roofs.

Swallow

Seen April to October. Look
for it twisting and turning
in the sky as it hunts insects.

Swallow's long, forked tail has
thin, streamer-like feathers.

Pheasant

When startled, rockets into
the air, calling 'kok, kok, kok'.
Female is speckled brown.

Yellowhammer

Likes open country. The rhythm of its song sounds like 'a little bit of bread and no cheeeese'.

Forms flocks in winter.

Skylark

Male flies straight up to a great height, hovers, and sails down, singing with a clear warble.

Female has a bubbling call.

Cuckoo

Listen for male's falling 'cu-ckoo' call. Found all over Europe in summer.

Owls and night birds

Short-eared owl

Looks fierce. Hunts in open
country in daylight and
at dusk. Perches on
ground.

You can't see its long 'ear' tufts while it flies.

Long-eared owl

Hides in branches in thick
pine woods. Hunts at night
and sleeps in the day.

Barn owl

Flies low over fields at night,
hunting small mammals.
Its call is a shrill shriek.

Nests in old buildings or hollow trees.

Nests in tree-holes.

Little owl
Small, flat-headed owl bobs up and down when curious. Flies low over farmland and hunts at dusk.

Tawny owl
Hunts at night around woods or old trees. Male calls, 'whoo, tu-whoo'. Female answers, 'tu-whit'.

Nightjar
Visits heathland in summer. Hunts insects at night. Churring two-note call.

15

Water birds

Mallard

This duck lives on rivers, canals ponds and lakes. Male makes sof 'crrb crrb' sound. Speckled brown female calls 'quack quack'.

Moorhen

Look for red bill and white tail. Makes 'kreck-kreck-kreck' and 'kyorrl' calls. Lives near ponds, lakes or streams.

Mute swan

Very large bird that lives by lakes or rivers. Hisses and flaps aggressively to protect its territory. Young swans are brown.

Kingfisher

Small with bright, shimmering feathers. Dives for fish in lakes and rivers. Listen for its shrill whistle.

Canada goose

Look in parks for this large goose with a noisy, honking call.

Grey heron

Often stands near rivers or lakes waiting to spear fish with its sharp beak.

17

Wading birds

Oystercatcher

Usually seen near sea, especially in winter. Feeds on shellfish.

Golden plover

Breeds on upland moors. Found in flocks on coastal marshes or lowland farms in winter.

Curlew

Nests on moors and upland farms. Seen on coasts at other times of year. Song is 'courli'.

Common sandpiper

Visits upland streams and lakes in summer, and wet, lowland areas in spring and autumn. Wags tail and bobs.

Looks black and white from a distance.

Lapwing

A farmland bird that forms flocks in winter. Displays in the air in breeding season. Call is 'pee-wit'.

Dunlin

Often visits the seashore, but nests on moorland in the north. Frequently seen in flocks.

19

Birds of prey

Peregrine falcon

Breeds on sea cliffs or inland crags. Dives on flying birds at record-breaking speed.

Buzzard

Large with broad wings. Often soars over moors and farmland as it hunts. Listen for its 'mew' call.

Kestrel

Hovers when hunting, often by motorways. Some nest in towns.

Red kite
Found in woods near lakes and open fields. Soars for long periods of time.

Look for deeply forked tail.

Sparrowhawk
Hunts small birds along hedges, woodland edges and sometimes in gardens. Never hovers. Female is larger and browner.

Golden eagle
Large, with long wings and tail. Found in the Scottish Highlands. Glides for long distances.

Spotting chart

Once you've spotted a bird from this book, find its sticker at the back, and stick it on this chart in the space below its name.

Barn owl	Blackbird	Blackcap	Blue tit	Bullfinch
Buzzard	Canada goose	Carrion crow	Chaffinch	Coal tit
Collared dove	Common sandpiper	Cuckoo	Curlew	Dunlin
Dunnock	Feral pigeon	Golden eagle	Golden plover	Goldfinch
Great spotted woodpecker	Great tit	Greenfinch	Green woodpecker	Grey heron

House martin	House sparrow	Jackdaw	Jay	Kestrel
Kingfisher	Lapwing	Little owl	Long-eared owl	Long-tailed tit
Magpie	Mallard	Moorhen	Mute swan	Nightingale
Nightjar	Nuthatch	Oystercatcher	Peregrine falcon	Pheasant
Pied wagtail	Red kite	Robin	Short-eared owl	Skylark
Song thrush	Sparrowhawk	Starling	Swallow	Swift
Tawny owl	Treecreeper	Willow warbler	Wren	Yellowhammer

Index